Rachael   Feb 16 - 2022
My Love to you this
special day Love you Meme

My prayer for you is that
you will always know that you are
loved, supported, and appreciated…
because you are.

ISBN: 978-1-59842-834-6

∏ and Blue Mountain Press are registered in U.S. Patent and Trademark Office. Certain trademarks are used under license.

Printed in China.
First Printing: 2014

⊕ This book is printed on recycled paper.

This book is printed on paper that has been specially produced to be acid free (neutral pH) and contains no groundwood or unbleached pulp. It conforms with the requirements of the American National Standards Institute, Inc., so as to ensure that this book will last and be enjoyed by future generations.

Blue Mountain Arts, Inc.
P.O. Box 4549, Boulder, Colorado 80306

My Prayer for You

Heartfelt Wishes of Hope,
Love, and Encouragement
to Show Someone You Care

Donna Fargo

Blue Mountain Press™
Boulder, Colorado

I Ask God to Bless You Every Day

Bless you for being you. Bless you for inspiring others with your kindness and for caring enough to lift people up and accept them without judgment.

Bless you for your compassion, consistency, and understanding. You believe the best of others and actually do what you believe. You live your life by example and practice the Golden Rule.

Bless you for celebrating every triumph, for consoling and comforting and sharing the pain of those who hurt. There is no ill will in your heart, no room for selfishness or resentment. You guide and enlighten, and you bring out the good in others.

Bless you for your strength and perseverance. In the face of adversity, your courage embodies wisdom, humanity, dignity, and a spirit of inclusiveness.

May your rewards be great, and may all the love you give out be returned to you. May you continue to be a bright light of hope and positive energy in this crazy, mixed-up world.

What a
Wonderful Gift
Your Life Is!

I hope you appreciate your talents and achievements and are thankful for how far you have come. As you look forward to the wonders waiting around every corner, I hope you embrace all the possibilities and make well-thought-out plans for your future. You are worthy, so claim your potential with confidence and enthusiasm.

Value your uniqueness and realize you're an angel in disguise to some, a friend so important to others, and a member of a family with whom you have significance and importance beyond description.

For every burning question you have, I hope you can find the answer and know that you're up to any task. If there are lessons you need to learn, trust that they will bring you closer to all you want to achieve.

We only get one trip through this life, so I hope you will choose to celebrate every day with all your heart.

I Wish You God's Favor and Good Fortune

We open ourselves to God's blessings when we acknowledge Him. May you feel the reflection of His light, His love, and His inspiration. And may you have the support and appreciation of those who are closest to you.

May your thoughts and actions be in sync with your abilities so you can have the life you desire and deserve. May you do everything you need to do to stay healthy and happy and be the best that you can be.

I wish you hope and faith to see you through every problem and help you make your dreams come true. May you never lose either of these as you work to reach your goals.

If you have love, good health, and hope and faith, there's no way you won't have happiness, success, abundance, and satisfaction in your soul. And because you stay close to God, everything will work together for your good.

You Are So Special...
You Are So Loved

You have such a gentle spirit. You understand and want to help. You love on purpose, and your intention shows. You refuse to judge others, and as a result, you make people feel accepted and equal.

You are guided by a sense of fairness and compassion that is not only right but also smart. You rely on compromise and cooperation to resolve conflict and ultimately improve yourself. You are an example, and you have earned the admiration and respect of others.

Because you trust humbly but deliberately, you are able to defy the odds and inspire miracles. Keep on being you. You are so special and so loved.

I Thanked God for You Today

Today, I thanked God for you and expressed my appreciation for your presence in my life. I said a prayer of gratitude for your loyalty and thoughtfulness and generosity.

I wished you an abundance of all the things that matter most to you. I prayed that you would have the kind of faith and wisdom you need to accomplish anything and everything you desire.

People who enrich our lives are such a blessing. I consider you a treasure that I would never want to lose.

I thanked God for you today.

You Can Make It Through Anything

Life is full of surprises — some good and some not so good. When your world gets turned upside down, do not despair. Try to look at what you're going through as a challenge rather than a struggle, as a time to develop patience, and as an opportunity to gain confidence in yourself.

Realize that you can choose your attitude even if you can't alter your circumstances. Put your opinions and feelings in perspective. Don't let them cause you to give up.

Do something for yourself to inspire courage and tenacity. Allow your life experiences to teach you what you want to know so you can move on. Don't be afraid.

Remember… just as there are clearer skies and brighter days after a hard rain, the stormy weather in your life will not stay. Life hurts sometimes, but you can make the best of any situation. In difficult times, you can find ways to handle disappointment, you can learn valuable lessons, and you can discover strengths to empower you. Life has its seasons, and you can make it through anything.

Even with All the Problems in Life, Never Lose Sight of the Good

The world is changing fast all around us, and sometimes it seems like there is nothing we can count on. But remember that there are some good things that will always stay the same.

God is still our Father, and He'll never leave us no matter what is going on in our lives. When we ask Him, He forgives and forgets, even when we hold things against ourselves. Love is still the best answer, and good always outweighs the bad, although rewards may not pay off according to our preference. And never forget the spiritual law that you can have what you want if you believe you can have it. If God is the same yesterday, today, and forever, then the rest is up to us.

We hold our future in our hands with every choice we make and every word we say. We can overcome or be defeated, give up or keep on trying. We can still choose right from wrong, good from bad, and we all know the difference. The Golden Rule always works, and if we follow it even when it's not easy, we develop the kind of integrity that matters. Each day we're making cumulative footprints on the stairway to our destiny, whether consciously and intentionally or not. Because we have the gift of free will, we are able to make choices that help us rather than hurt us.

God hears and answers prayers when we have faith that He will, but it is often a cooperative effort rather than a miracle dropped into our lap. As long as we are doing our part, we can always count on God to do His.

Believe in the Power of God's Love

When you're down, believe that this is just a place you're in and that you won't be discouraged forever. Believe that your body, mind, and spirit are on your side, and don't let this disappointment define you. Besides, this may be a divinely inspired detour that will benefit you in the long run.

When you're confused, believe that clarity will come when you're ready to move forward. After you've done all you know to do, believe that God is working out the details so you can be blessed. With awareness, you will gain knowledge, so trust that your day will come in perfect timing.

When life's not fair, you can still choose to be hopeful and faithful. No matter what you're experiencing, you don't have to let anything steal your joy. You will always have some advantages that others may not have. Believe that God loves you and He gave you your dreams, your vision, and your purpose — and remember that all things are possible for those who are willing to put their faith into action.

Trust in God
No Matter What

It takes strength and wisdom to believe in something you can't see. It takes determination on your part to refuse to give up when the cards are stacked against you.

When you feel so dejected that hope will not come to your rescue and words land only on deaf ears, you must fill up your cup with spiritual thoughts based on a higher authority than yourself. Do all you believe you should and trust in God.

Shine out every dark corner with the light of God's word. Meditate on certain scriptures and believe they are personally true for you. Speak your desires silently and aloud as though they are already accomplished, with a sincere "thank you" attached. Plant the seeds of God's word in everything you do. Allow yourself to dream and believe in the impossible. Don't let yourself be consumed by misery and discomfort. Don't believe anything that tries to make you think that things will never get better. Let your thoughts and actions demonstrate your faith. Trust in God no matter what.

Focus on the Positive

You're a very important person to so many —
you matter to God, to yourself, and to everyone
who loves you.

Consider all the good things in your life and be
grateful. Lay down anything that weighs on you
and decide to make every day special.

Most of all, focus on what you have today...
what you can do, how fortunate you are, and
how thankful you are for the people in your life
who are important to you.

Happiness is your birthright, but only if you want it to be. It's the feel-good part of emotional and spiritual health. It is the dessert of life without the calories. You deserve to have a well-rounded life, and happiness provides the building blocks that are good for you. If you're not happy, you're cheating yourself.

Celebrate every minute of life. Don't waste your time here. It's just too precious. You are a child of God, and your spirit, dreams, and purpose have behind them the most powerful energy you can imagine. The possibilities are limitless. Be as amazing as you want to be, and always thank God for your blessings.

Listen to Your Heart

Your heart is listening and talking to you. It hears everything you say, knows everything you do, and feels everything you're feeling. It knows your secrets and regrets, faults and assets, weaknesses and strengths. It remembers your background and the influences other people have had on you. It knows your habits, your deepest desires, and your proudest moments. It wants to help you. It will make suggestions to you in a still, small voice that may come to you in unexpected ways, like something you just happen to hear or see or read. Sometimes you may want to ignore it because you think your mind will have better advice, but your heart will never steer you wrong.

Trust what you hear when your heart is talking to you. It holds your hopes and dreams. But it is not an inactive guardian or an idle keeper — it feels your hunger and understands your purpose in life. It can help you decide what to do to fulfill that purpose — the changes you need to make and the methods that will assist you in making them. It will collect all the options unique to you to help you make the best choices for your life. It will caution you and encourage you. It communicates with you through your intuition, and if you listen, it will help you find opportunities you never dreamed were possible. Practice listening to your heart, and don't be afraid to trust its guidance.

Three Steps to a Rewarding Life

First, have the right attitude. Look at your circumstances as life lessons. Into each life rain may fall, but you will never be given more than you can handle. Have the expectation that you are prepared for anything.

Besides, what's a little rain? You've been rained on before and others have too. You know to take cover. You have good common sense. You've learned how to deal with other problems. You're a survivor and you can do more than you think you can.

Second, live your life in a spirit of cooperation with others. Be as good as your word, and don't make promises you're not going to keep. Be considerate of other people's time. Show compassion and the true essence of who you are.

Third, plant your feet on solid ground. God is on your side and not against you, and you can do all things through Him. When something brings you down, pick yourself up. When you're wrong, ask forgiveness. When someone wrongs you, forgive. Treat others the way you want them to treat you. You cannot lose if you continue to respect life and the gifts you have been given and have nurtured. Your words and actions tell the truth of who you are.

With boundless energy and enthusiasm, look at each day as a new opportunity to do the things that are important to you. Be true to yourself and your values. Walk in love toward others, and you will have a rewarding life.

Love Is the Greatest Teacher

Love can make you feel like you are cradled in the arms of some mighty presence. It can seem almost like a dream — but you're fully awake and aware. It can inspire smiles in you to give away to those who need them. It makes you want to be a positive influence on others. It helps you live every moment mindfully and tells your worries to move on. When the world is looking dark, it becomes your guiding light. Even faith works by love.

In the eyes of love, you are understood and forgiven — and you also want to understand and forgive. There are no limiting conditions. Love won't force itself on you. It only goes where it's invited… to a willing heart and mind that want to embrace life as sacred and beautiful. As it becomes the guardian of your blessings, it melts away every shield you've put up to protect yourself from the slings and arrows of life.

The ability to love and be loved is a miracle we all carry inside us to enhance our own potential. One act of love at a time, each of us can make a difference. Love just makes life so beautiful. If we could only love enough, we could change the world. What a blessing love is!

Forgiveness Is
the Greatest Healer

Forgiveness is an act of love. It's a gift we give ourselves so God can bless our lives. He calls on us to forgive and not judge, to love and not hate. But He has also given us free will, so it must be our choice — an intentional act of the spirit to put us in charge of our own humanity.

We all have within us the potential to choose forgiveness. It's the one thing that is always the right thing to do. It heals any wrong that cries out to be healed, and it brightens the pathways of life. It breaks down self-imposed barriers and causes us to put ourselves in someone else's shoes.

Withholding forgiveness can be like a restrictive, burdensome weight on our soul. A loving spirit knows it doesn't have to hold on to the hurt someone else inflicts upon it — whether intentionally or accidentally. Forgiveness sets us free to realize that we can be in control and we can refuse to let resentment steal our joy.

As God's children, we are instructed to forgive others and ourselves. So let's love and let's forgive… always.

Always Keep a Dream in Your Heart

Think about who you desire to be and what you want out of life. Search your heart for the dreams that you're passionate about and the interests that drive you and excite you. Believe in yourself and be convinced that you can do anything you need or want to do.

Take some time to plan according to your purpose. Educate yourself, and become as much of an expert as you can so you'll be prepared to reach your goals. Listen to others who have "been there." Stay engaged and productive — don't let yourself be without dreams and wishes and hopes and something to look forward to.

Keep your heart and mind open. Make the process of learning fun. Don't be afraid to ask questions. Be informed, but remember that you can always learn something new about anything.

Your intuition is powerful. Use it, and don't be afraid to take careful chances. Live your life consciously; don't just let your life live you. In your mind's eye, create a positive picture that will draw what you want to you. Be your own best friend. Cheer yourself on. It's when your words and actions are in line with your dreams and goals that you will see your dreams come true.

Use These Keys to Help You Unlock Any Door

Faith… It is taking God at His word and believing your prayer will be answered. It's the step beyond hope. It's God's gift to His children.

Optimism… Choose your thoughts, or your thoughts will choose you. Know that you can do whatever you think you can.

Courage… It's the strength that comes to your rescue when it looks like all hope is gone. It's the kind of bravery that will help you overcome disappointment and perform the impossible.

Willingness… Sometimes it's hard to believe that you can really have what you want, but with a willing mind, you can train your spirit to use its authority to help you reach your every goal.

Imagination… The child within you needs a fantasy place to escape to sometimes. In the playground of your mind, you are free to explore your creative spirit without preconceptions.

Truth… When you're honest with yourself and others, you can avoid misunderstandings — and save yourself a lot of time.

Patience… Whether you possess it naturally or have to develop it, you need it. It's a quiet kind of confidence and a reward worth the wait.

Prayer… This is the great balancer. It's our direct line to God that connects us with His spirit. It is the key to His kingdom. It humbles us and keeps us strong.

Love… It's the greatest commandment: love God, everyone, and yourself. Faith works by it, and happiness is a result of it. Love makes your life more beautiful.

If you rely on these keys, they will give you the guidance you need to unlock any door.

Every New Day Is...

A *Gift of Life.*
Greet each day with a grateful countenance.
Imagine your future. Make some new plans.
Remember your uniqueness. Reflect on how
much you are loved.

A Present to Yourself.
Do something fun, special, magical, and
memorable. Pretend it's your very own holiday.
Appreciate your gifts. Recognize your talents.
It's really okay to concentrate on you sometimes.
Be thankful for what makes you you.

A Time to Celebrate.
The greatest gift you've been given is you.
Celebrate yourself... with hope, with joy, with
appreciation. Dare to dream. Open the door to
your imagination, and let yourself go as far as
your mind will take you. Drop any regrets and
negative thoughts that hold you down.

A Day to Be Happy.
Count your blessings; love your life; treasure
your family and friends and all that you're
thankful for. Above all, enjoy each moment
with all your being.

Every day is a new beginning.

Don't Ever Forget What a Treasure You Are

A treasure is something really special... something irreplaceable, something you wouldn't want to lose for anything... something you value highly, protect, and appreciate so much. The special people in our lives are treasures to us, and I want you to know what a treasure you are to me.

I can't think of anyone who could take your place. My world is so much better with you in it. Because of your presence in my life, I am more steady and balanced, more confident and secure. I appreciate you more than I know how to say.

You are such a rare and beautiful person, and I will always believe in you. I wish you answered prayers, fulfilled dreams, and the very best life has to offer. Nothing will ever change how much I care about you. Even though words seem inadequate, I want you to know that you are a treasure to me.

My Prayer
for You

Wherever you go, I pray that a band of guardian angels will watch over you and protect you and shield you from harm. I pray that you will take care of yourself, stay grounded in faith, and feel God's never-ending presence.

I wish you good health and happiness all the days of your life and the wisdom to deal with every challenge you face. There are no walls around my heart, and the door is always open to you. If love, good wishes, and prayers provide any guarantees, you are safe and secure and you will face life fearlessly and triumphantly.

I hope you will give yourself permission to roam freely in a universe of unlimited potential and possibilities — beyond regrets and disappointments — where reality is okay just as it is. Love your life and see it as a beautiful present from God. Find the joy in every day and have fun. When things aren't working out for the best, remember that you are strong and you can still make the best of whatever comes along.

My prayer for you is that you will always know that you are loved, supported, and appreciated… because you are.

About the Author

With her first album, *The Happiest Girl in the Whole U.S.A.*, which achieved platinum album status and earned her a Grammy, Donna Fargo established herself as an award-winning singer, songwriter, and performer. Her credits include seven Academy of Country Music awards, five Billboard awards, fifteen Broadcast Music Incorporated (BMI) writing awards, and two National Association of Recording Merchandisers awards for best-selling artist. She has also been honored by the Country Music Association, the National Academy of Recording Arts and Sciences, and the Music Operators of America, and she was the first inductee into the North America Country Music Association's International Hall of Fame. As a writer, her most coveted awards, in addition to the Robert J. Burton Award that she won for "Most Performed Song of the Year," are her Million-Airs Awards, presented to writers of songs that achieve the blockbuster status of one million or more performances. In 2009, the state of North Carolina named a highway after her, and in 2010, she was inducted into the North Carolina Music Hall of Fame.

Prior to achieving superstardom and becoming one of the most prolific songwriters in Nashville, Donna was a high school English teacher. It is her love of the English language and her desire to communicate sincere and honest emotions that compelled Donna to try her hand at writing something other than song lyrics. Donna's other books include *I Prayed for You Today* and *I Thanked God for You Today*. Her writings also appear on Blue Mountain Arts greeting cards, calendars, and other gift items.